Earl Grey

The Commercial Policy of the British Colonies and the McKinley Tariff

Earl Grey

The Commercial Policy of the British Colonies and the McKinley Tariff

ISBN/EAN: 9783337151423

Printed in Europe, USA, Canada, Australia, Japan

Cover: Foto ©Suzi / pixelio.de

More available books at **www.hansebooks.com**

THE COMMERCIAL POLICY

OF THE

BRITISH COLONIES

AND

THE McKINLEY TARIFF

BY

EARL GREY, K.G., G.C.M.G.

London
MACMILLAN AND CO.
AND NEW YORK
1892

TO THE PEOPLE OF THE DOMINION OF CANADA.

THE subject of the following pages is one which I regard as of extreme importance to the whole British Empire, but I dedicate them to you because I believe that the inhabitants of no other part of that Empire would gain so much by adopting the policy I have endeavoured to recommend as yourselves, or would suffer so much as you would do by clinging to the opposite policy in the present state of your affairs. Holding this opinion, I entreat you to give at least your serious consideration to the arguments I have advanced in this pamphlet for your rejecting the policy of giving what is called "protection to native industry" as being both opposed to common sense and to the teaching of experience, and for your adopting in its stead the policy of Free Trade. I would also call your special attention to the political as well as the economical advantages which

I have endeavoured to show would be gained by your taking this course.

My dedication to you of what I have written against the policy of imposing "protecting" duties adopted by several British Colonies, and the appeal I have made to you seriously to consider the arguments I have brought forward, have been suggested by the deep interest I have never ceased to take in the welfare of Canada since it was my duty nearly half a century ago to take an active part in the management of its affairs as Secretary of State for the Colonies, to which office I was appointed on the formation of the administration of Lord J. Russell in July 1846. One of the most pressing subjects the new Government had to consider on coming into power was the very unsatisfactory state of affairs in Canada, and we came to the conclusion that in order to secure the peace of the Colony it was necessary to entrust its Government to a person of greater political experience than Lord Cathcart, who had recently been appointed to the office of Governor-General, principally, as we had reason to believe, in order to unite the chief civil and military authority in the hands of the General commanding the troops while the dispute with the United States on the Oregon question was still unsettled. Accordingly, with the concurrence of my colleagues, I recommended Lord Elgin to the Queen for the office of Governor-General, though he was at that time personally unknown to me, and though during the short time he sat in the House of Commons he acted with the party opposed to our own, because the manner in which he had conducted the government of Jamaica pointed him out as being singularly well qualified for the arduous post he was selected to fill. Before he proceeded to Canada to assume its duties we had ample opportunity for discussing the principles on which he ought to act, and it was satisfactory to find that our views on the subject were the same. While I continued in office I kept up a constant confidential correspondence with him on all his measures in addition to that of a more public character, and in common with the other members of the Government strenuously supported his policy against the attacks made upon it in both Houses of Parliament. Few of those who at this distance of time look back at the records of the proceedings I refer to will deny the factious character of these attacks, which very much increased the great difficulties he had to contend with. By the sound judgment and firmness he displayed, he happily succeeded in surmounting them, so that on the fall of the administration we left Canada in all respects in a far better condition than we had found it.

In 1846 extreme discontent was manifested by a large part of the population. In the beginning of 1852 their affections, which had appeared to be hopelessly alienated, had been regained, and all classes joined in evincing their attachment to the British Crown and to the institutions under which they lived ; the hateful animosities and rancour which had been created by civil war and differences of national origin had almost disappeared, and the party divisions which still existed were not greater than those usually to be found in all free governments. A system of constitutional government copied from our own had also been brought into full operation, and was universally acquiesced in. An equally marked improvement had taken place in the material prosperity of the Province, as was shown by the fact that its credit in the London Stock Exchange had risen from a somewhat low level, and was fully as high as that of the United States.

I will only add that I beg you to believe me your very sincere and earnest friend and well-wisher,

GREY.

March, 1892.

THE COMMERCIAL POLICY OF THE
BRITISH COLONIES
AND THE McKINLEY TARIFF

THE COMMERCIAL POLICY OF THE BRITISH COLONIES AND THE McKINLEY TARIFF.

THE greater part of the following pages were written with a view to their being published in the *Nineteenth Century* for February as a sequel to an article I had contributed to that Review for the preceding month, but it was found to be impossible that they could be published in that manner, as what I had written with regard to the commercial policy adopted by the British Colonies far exceeded the length to which articles in the Review are necessarily restricted. Believing, however, as I do, that the policy adopted by these Colonies has been highly injurious to themselves as well as to the whole British Empire, and that its essentially erroneous character has not as yet been adequately exposed, I have determined to correct and expand what I had intended for the Review and publish it as a pamphlet. I do not forget that pamphlets but rarely have much effect on public opinion, but in this case the faults and the evil effects of the commercial policy which has been pursued appear to me to be so clear, and the advantages that would result from abandoning it to be so certain, that I am induced to do what little I can to call public attention to a subject I regard as one of high importance which has not yet received as much consideration as it deserves. It is of special importance at the present time from its direct bearing on the question the Imperial and Colonial Governments have now to deal with as to the action it would be most expedient for them to take with regard to the recent adoption of the McKinley tariff by the United States.

In order to make the following remarks more easily intelligible, I will begin them by stating that my chief object in the article in the *Nineteenth Century* for January, to which they are meant to be a sequel, was to recall to public recollection some of the main arguments now seemingly almost forgotten, by which in the great struggle of half a century ago the advocates of Free Trade urged the adoption of this policy as the best and surest means of relieving the nation from the financial and industrial difficulties it was labouring under when this struggle began. I further pointed out that these arguments eventually convinced both Sir R. Peel, who had been the ablest supporter of a protectionist policy, and also the great majority of the nation, that the policy of the free

traders ought to be accepted, and that under this
policy the trade and industry of the country had
flourished beyond all former experience, and beyond
the expectations of the most sanguine free traders.
In one respect I admitted that these expectations
had been disappointed since the example of this
country had not had the effect that had been
anticipated in leading other countries to adopt
a commercial policy of the same character as that
which had here proved so successful. This failure
however, I contended, was to be accounted for by the
fact that one of the most important principles of our
commercial policy of 1846 was practically abandoned
when a bargain was made with France by the treaty
of 1860 for alterations in the customs duties levied by
the two nations on each other's produce in direct
violation of the rule previously acted upon that our
duties on imports were to be imposed for revenue
only, and that their amount was to be determined
solely by a consideration of what was best for our own
financial interests without reference to the terms on
which foreign countries admitted British goods to
their markets. I gave reasons, of which I believe the
force cannot be successfully disputed, for holding that
the violation of this rule by the treaty with France of
1860 had been a great mistake, and had contributed
more than any other single cause to create a belief in
other nations that this country had ceased to have

the same confidence it had formerly professed in its
commercial policy of 1846, and to produce that
general reaction of foreign opinion in favour of the
opposite policy of protection which has undoubtedly
taken place since 1860, and has made almost all commercial nations unwilling to admit foreign produce to
their markets except on the condition of what is called
" reciprocity." From this recapitulation of the con-
clusions on the subject of commercial policy which I
sought to establish in the *Nineteenth Century* for
January, it may be observed that in the article re-
ferred to I confined my attention almost entirely to
the effect in the United Kingdom of the changes
made in this policy since the beginning of 1846. I
will now endeavour to show that the system of free
trade adopted in that year proved beneficial to the
whole British Empire, and that the subsequent entire
abandonment by some of our principal Colonies
of this policy in order to adopt one of protection has
caused much more serious evils than even the mistake
made by the British Parliament and Government in
1860.

In the earliest days of the establishment of British
Colonies it was held that the main advantage to be
derived from possessing them consisted in the trade
we could carry on with them, and that to secure this
advantage it was necessary to make them conform to
the policy of the mother-country in all that relates to

trade. They were accordingly required to submit for
its benefit to severe restrictions on their trade with
the rest of the world, which were a great obstacle to
their industrial prosperity. After the American
revolution and in the early part of the present
century the restrictions on colonial trade by Imperial
legislation were much diminished, but they continued
to be no slight obstacle to its development up to the
time when Parliament adopted the policy of Free
Trade. But though these restrictions had originally
been highly impolitic and vexatious, and continued to
be injurious so long as they retained any of their first
character, I cannot doubt that it was wise to insist
that the commercial policy of all the British
dominions should be conducted on one uniform
system, with a view to the general benefit of the
whole Empire, and that the Imperial Parliament
should retain in its own hands authority to decide
what that policy was to be. When the system of
Free Trade was adopted no question had ever been
raised as to its being right to maintain this authority
of Parliament (though on some occasions the wisdom
with which it was exercised was disputed), nor was it
imagined by any one that it was to be relinquished
because the new policy of relieving trade from
injurious restrictions was to be adopted. It was, on
the contrary, assumed by all parties as a matter of
course that the commercial policy of the Empire

would continue to regulate as heretofore all measures relating to the trade of the Colonies. Accordingly while they were relieved from highly inconvenient regulations by the repeal of the Navigation Laws, and from the obligation of giving artificial encouragement to British trade by taxes on foreign goods, they were deprived of the privilege they had enjoyed of having some important articles of their produce admitted to our markets at lower rates of duty than those charged on the same articles when imported from foreign countries. The Royal instructions which had for many years forbidden the Governors of all Colonies having representative legislatures from giving the Royal assent to any Acts passed by these legislatures for imposing differential duties on goods imported continued to be enforced, and in 1850 Parliament, in extending the system of representative government in the Australian Colonies, strictly prohibited the imposition of any such duties by their legislatures. By introducing these provisions into the Australian Government Act, which gave large powers of taxation to the legislatures, Parliament clearly manifested its determination that allowing trade and industry to flow in their natural channels, without being artificially diverted into others, was to be the future policy of the whole British Empire, and not merely that of the United Kingdom.

The effect of thus relieving the Colonies from the

restrictions by which their trade and industry had
been previously hampered and misdirected was highly
satisfactory. In the first instance, the change of
system inevitably produced no little inconvenience
and alarm (though care was taken to mitigate the
inconvenience by allowing reasonable delay in bringing the change into full operation) : but when these
temporary difficulties had passed away all the British
Colonies began to advance rapidly in prosperity, with
the exception of those which still continued to suffer
from the injudicious manner in which the inevitable
and righteous measure of abolishing slavery had been
accomplished some years before. Some even of the
former slave Colonies were showing that in spite
of the very faulty character of the Act of Emancipa-
tion, as well as of the loss of the monopoly formerly
granted to their sugar in the home market, they
were deriving real benefit from the greater freedom
which had been given to their trade. The absence of
any signs of similar improvement in others of the
sugar Colonies was partly at least owing to the
persistent opposition offered by the great body of
those interested in West Indian property to all the
measures of the Government, in the vain hope of thus
compelling it to restore the Protection against foreign
competition in the English market which colonial
sugar had formerly enjoyed. The planters failed in
their real object of extorting that concession from

the Government, but greatly to their own loss they succeeded in preventing the adoption of most of the measures that were contemplated for the purpose of correcting, as far as was still possible, the evils caused by the failure of the system of apprenticeship, which had been relied upon for the means of keeping up a supply of labour for the cultivation of sugar when slavery was abolished.

With this partial exception the British Colonies showed by their rapid advance in wealth and prosperity that they, as well as the mother-country, had gained largely by their being relieved from the restraint of laws passed for the purpose of artificially directing their industry and trade into other channels than those into which they would naturally flow if left to themselves.   But favourable as they were, the results obtained by adopting the policy of Free Trade did not satisfy the inhabitants of the most important of the Colonies enjoying representative institutions. Popular opinion in most of them began after a time to be declared in favour of adopting the system of "protecting native industry." Yielding to this popular opinion, the Ministers who have held power in this country during the last five-and-twenty or thirty years have, by successive steps, allowed (unwisely as I think) the commercial policy for our Colonies which had previously been established by Parliament to be completely reversed.   This change has been effected by allowing the assent of the Crown to be given (contrary to all former practice) to Bills passed by the colonial legislatures for imposing duties on imports avowedly for the purpose of protecting various colonial goods against foreign, and often also against British competition, and thus directly violating the main principle of the Imperial policy of Free Trade. By allowing these Acts to receive the Royal assent, the Ministers of the Crown practically put an end to the ancient and most important rule of our colonial administration, that there should be one uniform system of commercial policy for the whole of the British dominions, which Parliament had plainly signified its intention to maintain when the system of Free Trade was substituted for that of Protection.

This surrender of authority by the Imperial Government, and the consequent abandonment by several important British Colonies of the Free Trade policy of the Empire in order to adopt that of protection, has, I believe, been injurious both to the whole Empire and to these Colonies. To the Empire, besides having been injurious in another way to which I shall presently refer, it has done serious harm by confirming the unfortunate belief created by the French treaty of 1860 that England had ceased to have confidence in its policy of 1846. To the Colonies it has done much more serious injury. Upon more than one occasion I have called attention

B

to the fact that in the long and earnest controversy
on the question of Free Trade, which was carried on
in this country half a century ago, the conclusion was
at length established in the opinion of Parliament and
of a great majority of the nation, that the real effect
of protecting duties is to lay a heavy burden on the
public without producing any corresponding revenue,
and to diminish the productive power of labour and
capital in the nations which resort to them.   I have
also shown that the effect produced by getting rid of
the protective duties formerly levied on many articles
of general consumption, in relieving British consumers
and at the same time increasing the revenue, has
afforded ample proof that Parliament was right in the
conclusion it came to.   Still I do not deny that in
fully peopled countries, where the work of improvement has been carried on for years, a want of
employment for labour and capital may sometimes
appear to exist, which affords plausible though (as I
am convinced) altogether unsound arguments in
favour of protecting duties.   But in all our most
important Colonies even this excuse for the policy of
Protection cannot be offered ; in them the want is not
of sufficient means of employing labour and capital,
but of an adequate supply of both, to turn to account
the great natural advantages they possess.   In such
a state of things it is surely a mistake, almost amounting to insanity, to divert industry by artificial

regulations from the employment in which it would be most productive, and to offer a premium at the cost of the community to those who will undertake to supply some of its wants by a greater expenditure of money and toil in work at home than would be sufficient to provide the means of paying for an equal supply of the articles it requires if imported from abroad. To see how contrary this is to common sense, we have only to consider what would be the effect of acting on the same principle in private life. Suppose, for instance, that a farmer or manufacturer who could find profitable employment for all the capital and labour he could command in his proper business were to grudge the money it would cost him to buy the tools and machines he required to carry on his trade, and were to resolve to make them for himself by diverting several of his hands from their usual work to this employment, though what he got in this manner would really cost him much more than the same things if he had bought them. He certainly, would become, not richer, but poorer by his folly, and would very likely end by getting into the "Gazette." When a Colony possessing rich natural resources, but insufficient means of turning them to account, compels by protecting duties a larger proportion of its capital and labour to be employed in producing at home articles it wants than would be required to procure an equal supply of them by importation, it acts precisely like the farmer or manufacturer in the imaginary case I have put, and like him must be made poorer by its folly.

Among various other bad consequences that have followed from the surrender by Parliament of its authority to maintain one uniform system of commercial policy for the whole Empire and from the consequent adoption by some Colonies of the system of Protection, one of the worst is that of its having tended to diminish, not only in these Colonies but throughout the whole extent of the British dominions, a sense of the community of interest which really exists among all the various members of the Empire, and which forms the only bond to be relied upon for keeping it together.

Several of the protecting duties imposed by the colonial legislatures have had the effect of preventing certain products of British industry from competing on equal terms with similar goods produced in the Colonies that have adopted tariffs containing such provisions, and this has not unnaturally created an angry feeling in the minds of merchants and manufacturers in this country whose trade has been thus impeded. They have considered the adoption of such measures by the colonial legislatures to indicate the existence in them and in the population they represent of a selfish jealousy of their fellow-subjects in the United Kingdom ; nor can it be denied that it was by no means unreasonable to regard it in this light. At the same time it has helped to foster, if not to create, those narrow feelings of commercial jealousy in the people of the Colonies it was here believed to indicate. And it is not only between this country and the Colonies but between the different Colonies with each other that feelings of animosity have been excited by the measures adopted in pursuance of the policy of Protection. A few years ago bitter (and just) complaints were made in Tasmania of the conduct of their neighbours in Victoria in imposing duties on the fruits of Tasmania to protect their own growers from their competition. There have been disputes of the same nature between Victoria and New South Wales, and between New South Wales and Queensland, and quite lately threats at least of a tariff war between Canada and Newfoundland. In this manner it is to be feared that feelings far from favourable to the maintenance of a firm union of all parts of the Empire must have been created both in this country and in the Colonies. I am glad, however, to believe that there is still a sincere desire that the Empire should be kept together, for I have of late observed with pleasure manifestations of a wish, both in this country and in the Colonies, for a closer union with each other. This I regard as a wholesome reaction against a very opposite feeling, of which I deeply deplored the existence more than forty years ago when it had been created and had gained somewhat alarming strength owing to the imprudent language and conduct of some leading politicians, who seemed to consider the maintenance of the integrity of the British Empire as a matter of little moment, and to believe that the right object to be aimed at in dealing with the Colonies was to reduce to a minimum the expense we incurred on their account, and our concern in their welfare.

I always held this to be a mistaken and mischievous view of what is the real interest as well as the duty of the nation, and I shall have to revert to the subject and give my reasons for so regarding it before I bring this paper to a close. In the meantime I will only say that I rejoice to think that after having been for some years apparently accepted as correct by a large number of our countrymen (including some of great political influence), the opinion I condemn seems now to be pretty generally repudiated, and to have given place to a much sounder one. This change of public feeling with regard to our Colonies affords iust grounds for much, but not for unmixed, satisfaction, since many of those who express the greatest anxiety to give additional strength to the ties that bind together the various members of the British Empire propose that measures should be resorted to for that object which I am convinced would prove, if adopted, injurious instead of useful.

One of the suggestions I allude to has so direct a bearing on the subject of this pamphlet as to make it proper that I should notice it somewhat fully. I refer to the scheme which has been put forward for seeking to establish a closer union between the mother-country and the Colonies by means of some change to be made in their commercial relations with each other, which it is asserted would confer great advantages on both, and which is to be effected by the aid of a body calling itself "The United Empire Trade League." This scheme is said to have received many promises of support, but its promoters have not yet laid before the public any clear and full explanation either of the precise nature of the change they desire to have made in our existing commercial system, or of the manner in which this change is expected to produce the promised advantages, though the need for such an explanation was very distinctly pointed out by Lord Salisbury to a deputation from the League which waited upon him some months ago. What comes nearest to the explanation which it is so necessary for the promoters of the scheme to give, if they have any confidence in it, is contained in some resolutions quoted by Colonel Howard Vincent, in a letter to the *Times*,[1] as having been passed in several of the Colonies in nearly the same terms, and expressing the opinion

[1] *Times* of the 25th of September last.

that—" The principles advocated by the United Empire Trade League, of preferential trading relations between all parts of the British Empire, will be of the highest individual and collective advantage." These words seem to imply a desire to return to the old system of seeking to encourage various branches, both of our domestic and colonial industry, by protecting duties and artificial restrictions ; but though it is difficult to attach any other meaning to the words, it seems incredible that this can be that which they are intended to bear. It is hardly to be supposed that it can be seriously demanded that the nation should revert to a system which was got rid of nearly half a century ago, because it was found to impose so heavy a burden on the Colonies as well as on this country, and when the experience of many years has now proved that its abolition has conferred very great advantages on all the parties concerned.

But if a return to the old system of colonial trade is not what the promoters of the League desire, I am at a loss even to form a guess as to any measures that could be adopted in the direction to which they point which would be of advantage to the Colonies. It must be remembered that we raise a very large revenue in this country by customs duties not one of which is of a " protecting " character ; they are all levied on articles which are either not produced at

home, like tea and tobacco, or if like spirits they are
produced at home, they are subject to a tax which
is regarded as equivalent to the duty on foreign
imported spirits, so that no advantage is given to the
home over the foreign producer ; we cannot afford
to dispense with the revenue thus obtained, or
permit the productiveness of the duties by which it
is raised to be diminished, by allowing colonial
produce to be brought into our market charged with
a lower duty than that paid by our own and foreign
producers ; still less could we consent to favour
colonial producers by charging duties from which they
should be exempt on the importation from foreign
countries of articles now admitted free.[1]

For these reasons it seems to be clear that no
attempt to draw closer the bonds of union between

[1] Since these sentences were written I have been told that it
has been suggested by some persons who declare their adherence
to the policy of Free Trade, that it might be well worth making
even a considerable economic sacrifice for the purpose of creating
some stronger bond of union than now exists between this
country and the other dominions of the Crown. With this view
it has, I understand, been proposed that in all the British
dominions 3 or 5 per cent. should be added to the duties levied
by them on such imports as come from foreign countries, and
that the produce of this tax should be applied as a contribution
to the expense of maintaining the Royal Navy. This scheme is
open to several obvious and fatal objections ; it is sufficient to
mention that it is essential for its success that it should be
adopted in all the British dominions, and the unanimous assent
to it of all the Colonies having representative institutions would
be little likely to be obtained. If it could, the imposition of
such a tax in the Colonies where the Crown has the power of

the several parts of the Empire by an alteration of
our commercial policy could possibly prove successful,
and I have no hesitation in expressing my firm
conviction that in order to attain this desirable object
we ought to look to measures in precisely the opposite
direction, and endeavour to induce the Colonies to
join with us in again adopting "in its full integrity"
the Free Trade policy entered upon by the repeal
of the old Corn Law in 1846, and completed and
successfully acted upon in the following years.

I am aware that owing to what has been done since
in a contrary sense, and to the present state of
colonial opinion, there is little or no chance that any
of our principal Colonies would now agree to give up
the policy of Protection, and as the Imperial Government acquiesced in, if it did not encourage their
adopting it, their departing from it could not now be
insisted upon. Still, the benefit they would gain from
a change of policy, as well as the loss and injury they
really suffer from that which they are now pursuing,
can hardly fail to become by degrees understood, so
that the day would probably come (though it might
not be an early one) when they would not refuse to
abandon their present system of diverting industry
from its natural channels, if earnest efforts were made

legislation, and in India, would involve too flagrant a violation
of the fundamental principles of the policy of Free Trade to be
sanctioned by any Government which is not prepared altogether
to abandon that policy.

by her Majesty's Ministers to bring about this result.

Though the Home Government and Parliament have thrown away the right of insisting that all her Majesty's dominions should conform to the commercial policy of the Empire, it is probable that the Colonies having representative governments (with which alone there could be any difficulty) might be led to recognize the expediency of doing so, and of abandoning the system of Protection as injurious to their true interest, by a judicious exercise of the authority and legitimate influence of the Ministers of the Crown.   Unfortunately there is reason to fear that this is not the use that will be made of their power and influence, since they have not shown signs of much earnestness in their support of the policy of Free Trade.   It is true they have disclaimed any wish to alter the fiscal system of the United Kingdom in the direction of a return towards Protection, and I have no doubt that no attempt to do so will be made, since it would meet with difficulties too great to be encountered.   But it is not enough that they should abstain from taking any retrograde steps; more is required in order to obtain for the nation the full benefits (which it has not as yet secured) of the policy of Free Trade.   For that purpose it is necessary that the conduct and language of the Ministers to whom the government of the country is entrusted should give unequivocal proof of their confidence in it, and of their determination to maintain it in its full integrity. They have been far from acting in this spirit. Even with regard to our domestic trade they have not declared with as little reserve as was to be wished their full adherence to the principle formerly acted upon by this country of refusing to discuss with foreign nations the rates of duty to be charged on its imports. With regard to the Colonies they have gone much farther, and have even encouraged them to look to the retention of their protecting duties, and to negotiation with other States for mutual commercial favours for the means of extending their trade. They have also abstained from all attempts to lead the colonial legislatures to conform to the commercial policy of the Imperial Parliament even when such attempts might have been made with advantage.

This remark applies especially to Canada, where the question has arisen whether any, and if so what, steps should be taken to guard British North America from the injury it is feared that it may suffer from the adoption by the United States of the McKinley tariff. This question has necessarily led to much discussion in the several provinces of the Dominion, and is one of very great importance not only to Canada but also to the Empire. It is much to be regretted that this discussion has been carried on in Canada with more of party spirit than of the calm reasoning which is required in order to come to a wise decision as to the measures to be adopted to promote the welfare of its people. During the late general election in the Dominion, a fierce controversy raged upon this subject, and I think it must have appeared to most of those who, like myself, watched its progress from a distance and free from any party bias, that those who were engaged in it on both sides have failed to give a sufficiently clear explanation of the policy each has striven to recommend to the electors, or to consider with enough care what would be the effect of adopting it. Thus on one side there have been frequent assertions of the necessity of establishing complete freedom of trade between the United States and Canada, but no account has been given of the arrangements by which it is proposed that this object should be carried into effect, nor do the difficulties that would have to be encountered in deciding upon such arrangements appear to have been seriously considered. Yet these difficulties would be great ; it is obvious that, if complete freedom of trade is to be established between British North America and the United States, the same duties upon imports must be levied in both territories, since, if they were not so, but higher duties were levied in the one than in the other, goods would be imported into that where the duties were lowest for

the purpose of being afterwards carried into the one
in which they were higher, which would thus lose part
both of the trade and of the revenue to which it
would be fairly entitled.   Canada, therefore, in order
to obtain the perfectly free intercourse with the
United States which is demanded by one party, must
consent to have its commerce with the rest of the
world, including the United Kingdom, regulated by
the revenue law of the United States, in settling
which it has had no part, and which may at any
moment be altered by a Congress in which it has no
voice.   The immediate effect of this would be to
subject the people of Canada to the heavy burden of
the new protective tariff of the United States, by
which many important articles of consumption are
subjected to extravagant duties, these being in some
cases intended to give artificial encouragement to
branches of industry not now carried on in the
Dominion, so that they would tax its inhabitants for
objects in which they have no interest.   An oppres-
sive burden would in this manner be imposed on the
whole population of British North America, and a
great obstacle would be thrown in the way of the
extension of its trade with all other parts of the world
except the United States.

This is not the only difficulty that would be met
with in establishing a Commercial Union between
these States and Canada.   Another very serious one

would arise in finding means for securing to each of the parties concerned its fair share of the revenue derived from the customs duties to which both would be subjected.   At present it is to be remembered that the revenue derived from these duties in the United States is appropriated by Congress (not by the State legislatures) to purposes which concern the whole Union, such as the maintenance of the army and navy, the expense of the Federal Government and of the diplomatic service, with various other charges of like character.   The several States which compose the Union have not, as such, any control over the expenditure of the large revenue levied from their inhabitants by duties on imports.   The formation of a Commercial Union between the Dominion and the United States would involve the necessity of paying the money received for duty on goods consumed in the Dominion into one fund with the customs duties levied in the States, since many of the goods intended for Canadian consumption would be sent through them, and pay duty in their ports, while on the other hand some portion of the goods meant for consumption in the States would reach them through the ports of the Dominion, and pay duty there.   As it would obviously be impossible to distinguish at the ports of entry of either territory on which side of the frontier the goods there charged with duty would be consumed, the whole would have to be included in the general receipts from customs duties by the United States, and thus form part of the revenue of which the appropriation rests with Congress. But the population of the Dominion could not be asked to allow the produce of taxes paid by them to be applied to objects in which they have no interest, by an authority in which they have no share. Justice would require that some arrangement should be made for placing at the disposal of the Canadian Parliament such a proportion of the total revenue derived from customs by the whole Commercial Union as should fairly represent the share borne by the inhabitants of British territory of the burden of the taxes by which the revenue is raised.

It would be no easy matter to devise an arrangement of this nature which would be really fair to both the parties concerned, and still more difficult to suggest one that they would think so, and that would not become a fruitful source of irritation and disputes between two States politically independent of each other, but joined together in this strange commercial partnership. Even if it could be successfully started (which is not probable), it is scarcely possible that such a partnership could be long carried on in this manner, so that if the Commercial Union is to be established and maintained, its leading to a political union must be looked for. Some of the advocates of a Commercial Union, including the most energetic and consistent of their number, Professor Goldwin Smith, do not shrink from avowing that this would be the inevitable consequence of its adoption, but consider this to be no reason for rejecting the measure, but, on the contrary, an argument in its favour. This, however, there is reason to hope is not the view taken of the subject by the majority of those who have joined in the cry for complete freedom of commercial intercourse between the United States and the Dominion. What they seem generally to desire is the entire removal of obstacles to an unrestricted exchange between themselves and their neighbours beyond the frontier of what they respectively produce, without sacrificing their present position as forming part of the great British Empire. I believe them to be mistaken in supposing that their entering into a Commercial Union with the great adjoining Republic is compatible with their maintaining their political independence and refusing a complete junction with it. But though in this respect I believe them to be in error, I do not doubt that they are right in wishing for a large alteration and improvement in their trading relations with their neighbours, and I will presently endeavour to show that this might be effected in such a manner as to secure for them all that is really required for their benefit, without affecting their political position. Before however I attempt to do this, I must first

offer some observations both on the evil consequences
to Canada that might be expected to follow from its
consenting to be united politically as well as
commercially with the United States, and also on the
views as to what ought to be the commercial policy of
Canada which have been declared by the late Sir John
Macdonald and by the present leaders of the party of
which he was so long the chief.

If it were determined that what is now British
North America should become part of the adjoining
Republic, it is to be presumed that the provinces
which now constitute the Dominion would be formed
into two or three, or perhaps a greater number, of
separate States, each exercising the powers which are
reserved to the several States by the American constitution, being as regards matters of general interest
under the authority of the Federal Government of
the Republic. Each of the new States would of
course send its due proportion of members to the two
Houses of Congress, and would be entitled to adopt
such a constitution for its own government as it might
think fit. By this change British North America,
instead of forming as it now does a nation already
rising rapidly into importance, would fall back into
the condition from which it has emerged, of being a
number of separate States having no organisation to
enable them to act in concert with each other, either
in carrying on great public works such as those which

have been already constructed, or in making postal and other arrangements for their common benefit. For dealing with all subjects of this kind in which the concurrence of more than one State is required, the inhabitants of the new States formed out of the Dominion would have to depend upon Congress and the Federal Government at Washington, in which their interests would command comparatively little attention. At the same time, the burden of taxation would be largely increased, as they would no longer have the revenue from customs at their disposal, and would probably have to provide for various expenses which are now met from this source by direct taxation. Their leading men, instead of having a political career open to them among their friends and neighbours in a government and legislature exercising large powers and dealing with important and interesting affairs, would only have a field for the exercise of their talents in the subordinate State governments, or in the distant Federal Government and in Congress at Washington, where they could only expect to hold an insignificant position in one or other of the parties which are there mainly occupied in the scramble for offices which is always going on.

Such would be the probable, I might almost say the certain, results that would follow to the people of British North America if their connection with the

Empire of which they form so important a part were
broken, in order that they might join the giant
Republic across their frontier; and another strong
reason remains to be noticed for their adhering to
what I rejoice to hear is the firm determination of the
great majority of their number to resist such a
change. Should what are now the several provinces
of the Canadian Dominion be formed into new States
of the American Union, their populations would be
involved in all its party contests, by having to vote
in the presidential elections and to return members to
Congress, and their whole system of government
would be assimilated to that of the older States of
the Union among which they would take their place.
But if the actual working of the American system of
government on the one hand is compared with that
of the Canadian Dominion on the other, as regards
the effects of each on the true welfare of the
populations which live under it, I think few impartial
and competent judges would hesitate in pronouncing
a decided opinion that the inhabitants of British
North America would be great losers by exchanging
their present system of government for a new one on
the American model. It would lead me too far from
my present subject to attempt a full explanation of
my reasons for holding this unfavourable opinion of
the American Government as it now exists, with the
various modifications it has undergone since the days

of Washington ; but I may observe that in the
United States what is the very first want of every
civilised society, that of having the law fairly and
firmly administered, is by the showing of the
Americans themselves very imperfectly provided for.
The tribunals in the United States fail to command
public confidence, either in criminal or in civil cases.
Tragic proof of the want of this confidence in the
administration of criminal justice has been afforded
. by the recent terrible scene in New Orleans, when a
number of Italians were put to death by a mob
without being allowed an opportunity of trying to
show their innocence of crimes imputed to them, and
of which as regards some of them at least there
seems to have been little if any evidence. The
language said to be often held by Americans about
their civil courts seems to imply a general belief that
suitors in them cannot rely upon them in having
justice done to them against wealthy and powerful
adversaries. Both civil and criminal cases appear,
from such accounts as I have seen, to be dealt with
more efficiently and more impartially by the Canadian
tribunals, and they command accordingly greater
public confidence. In the territory under their
jurisdiction men have·never, so far as I am aware,
been put to death without trial by " Lynch "—or, as
it might better be called, " Mob "—law, because the

firm administration of the regular criminal law cannot be relied on.[1]

In another respect the Government of Canada seems to show a marked superiority over that of the United States. Recent disclosures have proved that the Dominion has not escaped what has been the bane of free governments in all ages, the use of corruption in one or more of its innumerable forms for the purpose of obtaining political power. But though the abuses of which the existence has been brought to light by the late inquiry of the Dominion Parliament are very grave, they do not indicate such a general and deep demoralisation of the population, by the habitual use of corrupt influence in party contests, as that which has been produced in the United States by the presidential elections, since they have been conducted on the principle that "to the victors belong the spoils." This maxim, which was first proclaimed some half century ago, has since been very generally acted upon, and it seems to be now recognised as part of the regular system of the American constitution, that the transfer of power from one political party to another by the result of a presidential election should be followed by a corresponding transfer of the offices

[1] An article in the *Fortnightly Review* for January by Mr. W. Roberts on the administration of justice in America shows that the evil is far greater than I had imagined to be possible when the above was written.

of the Federal Government—the lowest as well as
the highest—from one set of men to another. This
practice, which if I am not mistaken is entirely
opposed to that which prevailed in the earlier years
of the American Union, has tended greatly to increase
the bitterness of party contests, by giving a large
proportion of the whole people a strong pecuniary
interest in the result of every presidential election,
which practically determines for the ensuing four
years whether the whole body of the civil servants
of the Federal Government shall be taken from one
party or from the other. It tends also to encourage
grave abuses in the conduct of these elections, since
when the battle has been won, and the "spoils"
according to the present practice have to be divided
amongst the "victors," the best shares in the booty
will naturally be assigned to those who have been
most active and successful (which unfortunately
generally means the most unscrupulous) in their
endeavours to secure it. Thus the majority of those
who fill offices in the public service under the Federal
Government may be expected to be extreme partisans,
who have earned their places by the zeal they have
shown in the election of the President by whose
authority these places have been given to them.
From men thus appointed, and who cannot reckon
upon holding their offices for more than four years,
it would be unreasonable to look for such an able or

such an honest discharge of their duty to the public as in this country we confidently rely upon obtaining from a body of experienced public servants who know that they practically hold their situations during good behaviour, and that unless they forfeit them by misconduct they will be allowed to retain them until they can retire upon the pensions to which in due time they will be entitled. Under the very different system which prevails in the United States, the civil servants, by whose aid the Ministers at the head of the various departments of the Government carry on its business, have not an opportunity of gaining that knowledge and experience which enables the permanent members of our public departments to render such invaluable assistance in managing the affairs of the nation, nor have they the powerful motive for abstaining from misconduct which is created by a knowledge that it will endanger their continuing to enjoy a secure provision for their lives. Instead of this the holders of subordinate offices in the public service of the United States are under a strong temptation to make the most of any opportunities their probably short tenure of their offices may afford of enriching themselves by improper means. We cannot, therefore, be surprised at finding, from time to time, in the intelligence which reaches us from America, indications that in the United States it is much less rare than in this country to hear of scandals as to dishonest gains alleged to have been made by those entrusted with the details of public business. The Republic must suffer greatly, both in its pecuniary and its moral interests, from the existence of such abuses, but though there appears to be a strong sense of the serious character of the evil among many of the best men in America, no effectual steps have yet been taken to abate it. The public in general, it must be presumed, has no wish for a reform in this matter, since it might easily be effected by a very simple law, but Congress has not been asked to pass one.

In maintaining that the Canadian people have now the advantage of living under a better system of Government than that under which they would be placed if they were to join the Republic of the United States, I do not mean to deny that Professor Goldwin Smith, in his late work on Canada and the Canadian question, has proved that there are great faults in the present constitution of the recently formed Dominion, and that it is not unreasonable to attribute to these faults the gross abuses that are shown to have taken place in its expenditure on public works. Admitting, as I must do, the force of the Professor's arguments as to the faults of the present constitution of the Canadian Government and their tendency to encourage political corruption, I entirely dissent from his conclusion that the Dominion ought to be broken up and its territory added as new States to the American

Union. On the contrary, I believe that by taking this course the population of that territory would exchange whatever evils they are now suffering from defects in the constitution and practice of their Government for greater evils of the same kind, that they derive great advantage from their union with each other and with the British Empire, and that what they ought to endeavour to accomplish is not a total change in their existing political condition, but such a reform in their institutions as may be found necessary in order to correct their faults without abandoning what is really good in them. And it is highly satisfactory to observe that the people of the Dominion seem to have exhibited with reference to the abuses lately discovered in the management of their affairs an earnest desire to guard against the recurrence of similar abuses in the time to come, very different from the apathy of their neighbours in submitting to the far more serious evils which notoriously arise from the prevalence of corruption, especially with reference to the presidential elections. It is earnestly to be hoped that judicious steps may be taken to accomplish the reform which has been shown to be so much needed in the Dominion, and I will venture to suggest that it deserves to be considered whether it would not be advisable for that purpose to appoint a small commission of able men, as free as possible from party bias, to inquire what are the real defects in the constitution of the Government of the Dominion and in its practical working, and to report to the Canadian Parliament their opinion as to how the faults they may discover might be best corrected.

Having thus endeavoured to explain the objections which may be urged, on political as well as on economical grounds, to the commercial union with the United States which the Opposition party in Canada has recommended as the best mode of guarding the Dominion from the evils it is considered likely to suffer from the new tariff of the American Republic, I must now attempt to show that what has been proposed by the Ministerial party for the same purpose is open to equal or nearly equal objections. In order rightly to understand these objections it is necessary to bear in mind what had been the previous commercial policy of the Canadian Government. When, several years ago, the late Sir J. Macdonald induced the Canadian Parliament to impose high protecting duties on various imports, he defended this measure not only because he held it to be desirable to encourage in this manner certain branches of Canadian industry, but also on the further ground that these duties were required in order to provide for the charge which would be thrown on the Treasury of the Dominion by the construction of the great public works he contemplated. These works, and especially the railway which was to create a new line of communication between the Atlantic and Pacific Oceans, would, he contended, confer great advantages on all the provinces of the Dominion by extending their trade and drawing closer their union with each other and with the British Empire ; but the cost at which these advantages could be obtained would necessarily be large, and could only be conveniently provided for in the manner he proposed. Though Professor Goldwin Smith has advanced arguments, which cannot be denied to have much weight, against the policy of imposing so heavy a pecuniary charge on the Dominion by constructing these works, the benefit already derived from them, and the prospect of still greater benefit likely to arise from them hereafter, lead me now to believe (contrary to what was my original opinion) that on the whole the measure has turned out to be a wise one, though I admit that there is still room for doubt on the subject.   Assuming it to have been wise to incur the expenditure, I do not dispute that Sir J. Macdonald was right in considering that the imposition of customs duties afforded the most convenient mode of providing the increase of revenue required to meet it, but I hold that a great and unfortunate mistake was committed when it was determined that these duties should be of a protective character.   When the policy of Free Trade was adopted in this country, it was not contemplated that customs duties should be given up

as an important source of revenue ; on the contrary,
it was one of the chief arguments of the early advocates of the abolition of Protection, that relieving
the country from those duties which imposed a
burden on the public without bringing in a corresponding amount of revenue would tend to increase
the amount received from the duties that were
retained. It was held that the essential principle of
the Free Trade policy consisted in abstaining from
all attempts to divert industry from its natural
channels, and in imposing taxes solely for revenue,
in such a manner as to take as little money as
possible beyond what was paid into the Treasury out
of the pockets of consumers.   This principle, it was
also held, would be fully maintained by acting upon
the rule that whenever duties were imposed on the
importation of articles of consumption, these articles
when produced at home should be subject to the
same amount of taxation.   This rule has always been
adhered to in this country since Free Trade was
adopted as the national policy.   If the same rule had
been followed by Sir J. Macdonald, and if he had
advised the Canadian Parliament to raise the
additional revenue that was required for public
works by imposing moderate customs duties of such
a character as to avoid inflicting any needless burden
on the consumers, the money that was wanted might
have been got with far less pressure on the popula-

tion than was caused by the protecting duties which were resorted to.

It is probable that his being already so deeply committed to what I have endeavoured to show was a mistaken commercial policy that induced Sir J. Macdonald to adopt the course he did, when the question arose as to how the adoption of the McKinley tariff by the United States ought to be met by Canada. If I understand correctly such of his speeches on this question as I have had an opportunity of reading, I find that while he denounced the project of his opponents to seek, either by a complete or only a commercial union with the United States, relief for the Dominion from the difficulties it was expected to suffer from this adoption of the McKinley tariff, he had himself nothing to suggest for that purpose except that an attempt should be made to enter into an agreement with the United States, by which each of the two Governments, while maintaining its general system of granting protection to native industry, should allow the free admission to its markets of certain imports from the other on the principle of reciprocity. For the success of this policy, to which I believe the present Canadian Ministers adhere, it would be necessary not only that there should be a disposition, of which there is no sign, on the part of the Government of the United States to come to a fair arrangement with Canada on this principle, but also that it should have the power of obtaining for it the sanction of Congress. The proceedings of that body on the McKinley tariff afford little ground for expecting that its assent to a law for giving effect to such an agreement would be easily or quickly obtained, more especially as it is hard to see what inducements could be offered to the United States for making commercial concessions to Canada. It may, therefore, be concluded that little or no hope of gaining any advantage in the manner suggested by Sir J. Macdonald can be reasonably entertained.

As any attempt to bring about an improvement of the commercial relations of Canada with the United States on the principle of reciprocity seems thus foredoomed to failure, and as the rival scheme of forming a Commercial Union is not more likely to succeed, there is surely good reason for seriously considering whether it would not be far better for Canada to follow the example of this country, by adopting the system of Free Trade with the same completeness that it was acted upon here during the first years after the repeal of the old Corn Law.

This is a question of such extreme importance to the welfare not only of Canada, but also of the British Empire, that, in the hope of obtaining for it some of the attention it deserves, I will endeavour to describe the advantages which I believe might be confidently expected to follow from the change of policy I have suggested. Before I do so I must, however, observe that if, contrary to what at present appears to be likely, the Parliament of Canada should be convinced of the expediency of the proposed change, and should determine to adopt it, I think it ought by some formal proceeding to record its reasons for taking this important step. I do not know how this could be more conveniently done than by its voting resolutions declaring its views, and in order to explain more clearly than I otherwise could the course which I would suggest for its consideration, I venture to give the following sketch of resolutions that might be proposed :—

Resolved : (1) That the new tariff of the United States will so materially affect the trade of Canada with these States as to render it necessary very carefully to consider what measures it is in consequence expedient to adopt to avert the injury which may thus be inflicted on the Dominion ; (2) That, looking to the whole course of the discussions in Congress on the new tariff, and to the communications since held with the Government of the United States by the Imperial Government, and that of the Dominion, there does not appear to be any reasonable ground for expecting that the United States can be induced to enter into a satisfactory arrangement for removing or mitigating the new restrictions imposed on the admission of Canadian produce to their markets ; (3)

That this being the case, it is inexpedient that the communications with the United States on this subject which have already taken place should be carried any further, and it would therefore be advisable that the Dominion of Canada should, without reference to what may be done by the United States, proceed at once to adopt such measures as may be found most likely to promote its own welfare ; (4) That with this view it is not expedient to impose new duties on produce imported from the United States, for the purpose of either excluding such produce from the market of Canada or diminishing the amount admitted, in retaliation for the increased restrictions imposed by Congress on importations from Canada ; (5) That the imposition of such retaliatory duties would add to any loss which the new American tariff may inflict upon Canada the further loss to its people of the supplies which they now find it to be for their advantage to draw from beyond their frontier, while no inconvenience to Canada can result from continuing to receive them ; (6) That it is, therefore, expedient that the Dominion, in order to avert any damage which the recent measures of Congress might inflict on its trade, should seek to create new openings for that trade in other quarters ; (7) That for this purpose it would be advisable to adopt the policy successfully acted upon by the British Parliament by abolishing, on the advice of Sir R. Peel and succeeding Ministers, all the protecting duties formerly charged on many imports into the United Kingdom, and levying only such duties of customs as may be required for raising revenue, and which do not impose any unnecessary burden on consumers; (8) That the adoption of this policy by the British Parliament having proved to be the means of greatly increasing the commerce of the United Kingdom and the welfare of the population, by relieving them from the burden of the former system of taxation, while it has largely augmented the productiveness of those duties on imports which are retained, it is expedient that the present Canadian tariff should be revised so as to make it conform in principle with the British tariff; (9) That the above resolutions be communicated through the Governor-General to her Majesty's Ministers, with a request that they will instruct the British Minister at Washington to intimate to the President of the United States that it is not considered by the Imperial Government, or by the Government of Canada, to be desirable that the rates of duty to be charged in the United States on imports from British territory, or in the British dominions on imports from the United States, should be made the subject of further discussion, or of any treaty or engagement between the two nations.

Proceeding now to explain my reasons for holding it to be certain that Canada would derive great advantage from the adoption of the policy indicated by these resolutions, I have in the first place to remark that the damage the Dominion could possibly suffer from the enactment of the McKinley tariff by the United States would be rendered exceedingly slight by merely avoiding the blunder of seeking to obtain a modification of the restrictions it has inflicted on Canadian trade, either by imposing retaliatory duties on American produce, or by entering into negotiations with the Federal Government for the reduction of the high duties now charged in the United States on Canadian produce. For reasons into which I need not now enter, I am convinced that an attempt to obtain a modification of the McKinley tariff by any such means would be a great mistake, and if this is avoided Canada would lose none of the benefit it now has in drawing from the States supplies for some of the wants of its population, and though the new restrictions of the McKinley tariff might interfere with the easiest mode of paying for these supplies, by giving Canadian produce in exchange for them, any inconvenience thus occasioned must fall chiefly on the inhabitants of the States, who are now deprived by that tariff of what they had hitherto found to be the best and cheapest means of obtaining some articles of consumption they require.   The merchants and money dealers of Canada may be safely trusted to find the means of paying directly or indirectly for all that may be purchased from the States for the use of the Dominion. The farmers and others in Canada who used to send a part of what they have to dispose of to the United States will now (as we are told) be deprived in a great measure of the market they have found there, but other markets would be open to them, and Canada is so rich in the various fields it offers for the profitable employment of capital and labour, that the worst that is likely to happen to those who have looked to the United States for a market for the produce of their industry is that they may have to make some change in the kinds of business to which they turn their attention.

Although I see no reason for apprehending that Canada will suffer any serious damage from the McKinley tariff, unless through some injudicious action of its own Government, I do not doubt that for a long time the people both of Canada and of the United States have lost much by having been debarred from free commercial intercourse with each other by unwise restrictions, and that relieving their trade from these artificial and mischievous hindrances imposed upon it by the fiscal laws of both nations would be one of the most valuable boons that could be conferred upon them. If the Parliament of the Dominion could be induced to abandon its present commercial policy for one of Free Trade, a great step would be made towards ultimately attaining this desirable object, as I shall presently endeavour to show ; but the more immediate advantages to be expected from such a change, and the urgent need there is for it, require to be first considered. The fact that there is an obvious and urgent need for an alteration of the present fiscal and commercial system of the Dominion has been proved by Sir R. Cartwright in his exceedingly able letter in the *Economist* of February 13, 1892, by evidence which seems quite conclusive ; and the evils he describes as now existing are most serious. His remarks on the connection there is between the terrible political corruption which to the great grief of its friends has been lately brought to light in Canada especially demand much attention, and even more is due to what he says as to the results of the recent census, since with regard to these he is speaking of matters of fact which cannot be disputed. He shows that, notwithstanding the very large number of emigrants who have been received in Canada, the increase of the population since the last census of ten years ago falls short of what might have been looked for from natural increase alone in a prosperous and thriving country. The inference is inevitable, that during these years the Dominion had not been prospering as it ought to have done, and that very many of its natives, as well as of the emigrants who have reached its shores, have been unable to find in it

homes in which they could enjoy such an amount of
welfare as to induce them to remain there. When we
consider what great natural resources and advantages
Canada possesses, it is difficult to see how this fact can
be accounted for, except by assuming that there must
have been some great fault in the management of its
affairs which has prevented the population from being
as well off as they have a right to expect and that
many of them have in consequence sought elsewhere
for better means of living than Canada has offered.

We may also fairly infer that the fault in the
management of Canadian affairs must lie in the fiscal
and commercial policy that has been acted upon, since
there has been no failure in maintaining order and
the security of person and property which usually
ensure prosperity to an industrious population. Why
the eminently industrious population of Canada has
not been more successful in reaching the prosperity of
which its many advantages held out a promise would
be inexplicable, were it not sufficiently accounted for
by the vicious system which, professing to give " protection to native industry," has really placed it under
conditions greatly diminishing its productive power.
Other facts to be gathered from the census and from
other sources of information afford further proof that
this is the true explanation of the progress of the
Dominion in the last ten years having disappointed
public expectation. Among these it is deserving of

special consideration that whatever increase of population has taken place in the Dominion has been mainly in large towns, while in some agricultural districts the number of the inhabitants has actually diminished. Even in the rich lands of the North-West, where great efforts have been made to encourage settlement, it has been far from being extended as rapidly as was looked for. The development of the mineral riches of districts where they are said to abound does not seem to be making greater progress than agriculture. These are significant signs of what are the effects of the present fiscal policy ; they appear to show that neither agricultural nor mining industry is, under present conditions, sufficiently remunerative to encourage the extension or the carrying on with spirit and energy of these great branches of national industry. The simultaneous increase of population in the towns, where the business of the protected trades may be presumed to be principally conducted, seems further to show that the burden of the taxes imposed for the purpose of affording this protection presses too heavily upon the industries which derive no benefit from it, and thus causes too large a proportion of the people, instead of bringing into cultivation the fertile land open to them, or improving that already cultivated, to resort to the towns in the hope of finding there a better return for their industry in the employments favoured by the existing fiscal laws.

This result of the system of Protection could hardly be regarded as favourable to the general and permanent welfare of the inhabitants of the vast territory included in the Dominion of Canada, even if it could be proved, which is exceedingly doubtful, that those engaged in the protected trades are really deriving from them the profit they have been led to expect. Already, if I am not misinformed, there have been complaints of losses sustained by those engaged in some of the protected trades in Canada, and that there should have been such losses is quite in accordance with the experience of other nations which have adopted the policy of Protection. The reasons for this are very obvious: though protected trades are not exposed to the free competition of foreigners, they have to meet that of their own countrymen, and when high protecting duties on certain articles hold out a prospect of obtaining more than the average rate of profit by producing them, there is generally a rush into the business of competitors for a share of the advantage, so that the rate of profit in the protected trade is speedily brought down to the average rate in other branches of business. It is often brought much lower. Whenever there has been a miscalculation as to the extent of the demand for any kind of protected goods, and more have been produced than can be sold without loss, no relief for the overcharged home market can be obtained by exporting the surplus goods to foreign countries, since the very fact that they require Protection at home implies that they could not meet the competition they would be exposed to abroad. Hence it has, I believe, been generally found that, in nations which have adopted the policy of Protection, it has seldom or never succeeded in securing for protected branches of industry steady and durable prosperity. One remarkable example of its having failed to do so in our own country occurs to me. When the manufacture of silk in this country was protected by the extravagant duties formerly charged on foreign silks, there were every few years most urgent appeals to the public for subscriptions to relieve the distressed Spitalfields weavers in the frequently recurring times of bad trade.

Perhaps it may be said that these arguments to prove that the policy of Protection has been injurious to the prosperity of Canada must be fallacious, since the United States have long acted on the same policy, and have of late carried it still further than Canada, and have nevertheless continued to enjoy industrial prosperity. This fact cannot be denied, but it must be remembered that the great American Republic enjoys several special advantages which have prevented it from suffering so much as it might otherwise have done from the policy it has pursued. The American Union possesses a vast territory, including a great variety of climates, and consequently able to raise a great variety of different kinds of produce, some of them (such as cotton and tobacco) of very great value, and which it has peculiar facilities for cultivating. There is absolute freedom of commerce between the States, so that internal trade in exchanging their produce with each other is carried on without obstruction, and almost supplies the place of foreign trade. The Union has also an immense capital invested in railways and industrial establishments of various kinds on a very large scale, a very considerable proportion of this capital having been drawn from this country by loans. With all these advantages, it is not wonderful that so energetic and clever a population as that of the United States should have succeeded in raising the nation to great wealth and prosperity in spite of its unwise policy ; and though it is true that the nation is in the enjoyment of great apparent prosperity, there are clear signs that this prosperity is not so great as it might have been under a different policy, and that it does not extend so widely among the general body of the working population as it ought. There are also signs of which Americans would do well to take timely notice, that at no distant time they may have to meet a much more serious competition than they have yet had to encounter in foreign markets for cotton and tobacco. In addition to other countries which already export both these valuable staples of American trade, it is highly probable that in a few years tropical

Africa may enter largely into this field of production, with its almost unlimited extent of rich soil adapted for such cultivation, and with its millions of inhabitants to whom its climate is congenial, and who have been found neither indisposed to industry when they have an assurance of reaping its fruits, nor incapable of useful labour under skilful guidance.   The African producers of cotton and tobacco are therefore likely to become very formidable rivals in the markets of the world to growers in the United States, especially if the latter continue to be hampered by the artificial difficulties with which their industry is now encumbered.

It is notorious that the cost of living, except as regards food, is very much higher in the United States than in any other country in the world.   House rent, clothes, and almost all the comforts and luxuries of life are exceedingly expensive, so that it is doubtful whether labourers, except the very lowest of the unskilled, are really as well off in spite of their nominally high wages in the United States as they are in this country.   We hear not unfrequently of English and Scotch emigrants who have been so disappointed in their hope of bettering their condition by leaving their native country, as to return to it after an experience of the homes they have sought.   Probably these cases would have been much more common if it were not so mortifying to a man to acknowledge by coming back that he had made a great mistake in emigrating, and, moreover, so difficult for him if he had given up a good position here to recover it on his return.

I cannot, therefore, admit that the apparently contrary experience of the United States disproves the truth of the conclusion I have endeavoured to establish, that the unsatisfactory progress in prosperity made by Canada in the last ten years is mainly owing to the unwise policy its Government has adopted with regard to trade and finance. The arguments in favour of that conclusion, both from reasoning and experience, remain in my judgment entirely unshaken, and if so, it follows that to abandon that policy for the opposite one which was adopted with such remarkable success by this country five-and-forty years ago is the right course for the Dominion to pursue. Nor is there any cause for alarm as to the distress which might for a time be inflicted on those engaged in the branches of industry now protected from competition. The new impulse given to trade by the proposed change of policy would add to the large field for the profitable employment of labour and capital which Canada possesses, and there would be little difficulty in finding means for turning to good account whatever amount of both might be driven from employments which would cease to pay when deprived of artificial assistance. The Parliament of Canada, if it should follow the example set by the British Parliament in adopting the Free Trade policy, would probably also

follow it by allowing reasonable time to those engaged
in protected trades to prepare for the change before the
new system was allowed to come into full operation.
In addition to the directly beneficial results which
I am convinced might be confidently reckoned upon
from the adoption of the policy of Free Trade in
Canada, I have already expressed my opinion that
it might probably prove the means of ultimately
securing another most important advantage, by
establishing far greater freedom of commercial intercourse than now exists between the Dominion and
the United States. No immediate reduction of the
duties levied in the United States on imports from
Canada can be looked for, but if Canada should adopt
a policy of Free Trade while the United States adhere
to one of extravagant Protection, it is impossible that
the difference thus created in the position of the
population on the two sides of the frontier line should
not produce before long a marked difference in
their condition, which can hardly fail to lead to
changes which are at present little thought of. In
some descriptions of produce British North America
and the United States are competitors in neutral
markets, and the high cost of living in the United
States, in consequence of the price of so many
articles of consumption being raised by protecting
duties, must give an advantage in these markets over
American producers to rivals who are not subject to

equal burdens. Hitherto producers in the United States have suffered little in this way in competition with those of Canada, because the latter have been subject to burdens of the same character as those inflicted on their rivals, though perhaps not to an equal amount. But if Protection should be abandoned in Canada, the cost of living in the Dominion, and that of raising there the produce which it has to sell in competition with the like produce in the United States in markets open to both, will be reduced so that the Canadian seller would have an advantage over the other. The enhanced cost, owing to protecting duties in the United States, of materials used in various trades would have a like effect, and already it has been asserted that the high duties now levied there on tinned plates will seriously raise the price at which American traders will be able to sell their canned fruits, and tend, therefore, to diminish the number of their customers in favour of Canadian produce.

Another result well worthy of consideration may be expected to follow from the admission into the Dominion, either duty free or subject only to a moderate duty imposed for revenue, of the many commodities charged under the McKinley tariff with evtravagant duties when imported into the United States. A great difference must thus be created between the prices at which such commodities would be sold on the opposite sides of the long frontier line which divides the territories of the two nations, and it is not likely to be long before enterprising traders discover that a good profit may be derived from setting up shops on British territory, in places to which American customers might easily resort to buy goods which are made artificially expensive in their own country. One example of the manner in which this may be done may be worth mentioning. Some time ago there were accounts in the newspapers of great distress inflicted on a large number of workpeople in Vienna by the prohibitory duty imposed by the McKinley tariff on mother-of-pearl buttons. It appears that the business of making these buttons for the American market has been carried on largely in Austria, with much advantage to those engaged in it, but that the new duty will prevent their being sold for less than two or three times their former price, and will effectually stop their sale. If this statement is true (which I see no reason to doubt), what is there to prevent traders from importing these buttons into the British North American territories (if they are there free from duty), and selling them at the old price to American tailors and dressmakers, and how could such customers be prevented from buying these things where they can be bought cheapest, and can be so easily carried across the frontier? Of course this would be smuggling,

which the Canadian Government ought not and I am
convinced would not encourage, but it would have no
right and no power to prevent Canadian traders from
offering cheap wares for sale in their own country, or
to forbid American customers from purchasing from
them what they want. It is the business of the
American revenue officers to prevent the introduction
of smuggled buttons or other goods across the
Canadian borders, a task which would become far
from a hopeful one whenever Canada adopted a Free
Trade policy and the United States adhered to one of
Protection. The inconvenience and loss the American
Government would certainly suffer from attempting
to maintain in its territory the existing scale of
prices for commodities under the McKinley tariff,
while a very much lower one was obtained under
Free Trade on the other side of the Canadian frontier,
together with the disadvantages under which the
population of the United States would soon find out
that they were placed as compared to their neighbours, whose industry was not encumbered by the
shackles of Protection, would in all probability
induce Congress before long to abandon its present
commercial policy, so far at least as to allow a far
freer intercourse between its own people and their
neighbours in British America than is now permitted.
This freer intercourse, which the Canadians so much
and so justly desire, would be far more likely to be

gained in this manner than by negotiation with the Government of the United States, which both the great political parties in Canada seem to look to look as the only mode of obtaining it. The experience of the civilised world, and more especially since the close of the great revolutionary war in the early part of the present century, proves that negotiations of this kind very seldom indeed lead to a satisfactory result, and as I have shown, there are special reasons for regarding any commercial negotiations between the British and United States Governments as almost sure to fail. But if, without asking anything in return (for this is an essential part of the policy), the Canadian Parliament were to set the example of abolishing all duties on imports, except such moderate ones as might be necessary for revenue, without excluding goods from the United States from admission equally with those from elsewhere, there would be a far better prospect of obtaining the desired object than would be offered by negotiation.

Nor is this the only reason for preferring the course I recommend. All that can be hoped from negotiations, even if they should not prove as abortive as is to be expected, is that they might possibly be the means of removing some of the worst obstacles to trade between the Dominion of Canada and its Republican neighbours, while both adhered to their policy of Protection. This would no doubt be a benefit to both parties as far as it went, but the advantages thus gained would not be likely to be of great importance, and would be insignificant as compared to those which would be secured if Canada should discard the system of Protection for the policy of Free Trade, with the same success that a similar change was made in this country, and if the eyes of the people of the United States should thus be opened to the heavy loss they really suffer by their excluding from their markets so large a proportion of the goods they might import with advantage from foreign countries. That such a change of opinion in the United States might follow from the adoption of a Free Trade policy in Canada is not only possible, but what I believe would most probably happen. Already there are signs that the absurdity of the McKinley tariff and the injury it inflicts on the nation are beginning to be understood. As yet the truth on this subject does not appear to be generally accepted by those who have not had opportunities of acquiring the knowledge necessary for forming a sound judgment on the question, and who form the great majority of the persons whose votes determine the policy of the nation, and therefore no immediate change in that policy can be looked for. But when the opinion that the Free Trade policy is right is already held by a large proportion of those competent to understand the question, and when its rejection is seen to lead to such manifest practical absurdities, it is sure to penetrate by degrees into the minds of a people who, though they may be uninstructed in the doctrines of political economy, are highly intelligent, and little likely to be long prevented from discovering that the fiscal system they have been persuaded to sanction flagrantly violates not only the principles of science but the plainest rules of common sense. This discovery can hardly fail to be made in the end, but it may probably be long delayed, unless it should be hastened, as I have given my reasons for believing that it would be, by Canada's adoption of the policy of Free Trade.

If the abandonment of the system of Protection in Canada should lead to such a change of opinion in the United States as I anticipate, and if in consequence freedom of trade should be established throughout the whole extent of North America, few, I think, will venture to deny that advantages of the very highest importance would be conferred on all its inhabitants, whether they live under the Imperial British flag or under that of the Stars and Stripes. Their character and circumstances, and the position of the two territories, create, as Professor Goldwin Smith has argued, so many common interests among those who reside on opposite sides of the national frontier, and such a need for free intercourse with each other, that to impede such intercourse between

E 2

them by artificial and needless obstacles is to commit a
folly as well as to inflict a serious injury upon both.
I heartily concur in this opinion of the Professor ; but
I must repeat my entire dissent from his conclusion
that the incorporation of British America in the
American Republic is therefore desirable. I hold, on the
contrary, that it is neither the only, nor by any means
the best, mode that could be adopted for removing the
obstacles that now impede the free intercourse which
ought to take place between them. If the customs
duties imposed by the two nations were confined to a
few moderate ones, not of a protective character,
charged upon articles of general consumption, in order
to raise what revenue might be required, and if these
duties were levied under judicious regulations they
would not practically interfere with that free intercourse which ought to be maintained. Assuming that
a proper arrangement were made for this purpose, it
would be far better for both populations that each
should be left to manage its own affairs independently
of the other, than that they should be joined together
in a union which could not easily be carried on without
giving rise to embarrassing and irritating questions.

In the Australian Colonies, their having no close
neighbour like the United States with which their
commercial relations are of vital importance, renders
the abandonment of the policy of Protection a matter
of less urgent necessity than it is in Canada, but still

there can be no doubt of the evils it is bringing upon them. Striking evidence that it is so is afforded by the following telegram which appeared in the *Times* of the 6th of February :—

"Melbourne, Feb. 4.

" A deputation from the suburban councils having represented to the Government that owing to the scarcity of employment thousands of men are starving, the Cabinet have admitted the seriousness of the situation and have resolved to start works.

" The revenue continues to fall, the decrease in the seven months of the financial year amounting to £400,000."

Such has been the result of a policy which professes to have for its object the benefit of " native industry " in a Colony so rich in natural resources as Victoria, and where it is admitted that these resources are very insufficiently made use of. Not only in ordinary agriculture in sheep-farming, and in mining, but also in various other kinds of production now either altogether neglected or obtaining far less attention than might be given to them with advantage, there is ample room for the profitable employment of more labour than is available. In a Colony thus richly endowed no need could have arisen for the Government to undertake the difficult and dangerous task of providing artificial and eleemosynary employment for labourers but for the unwise imposition on many articles of protecting duties which diminish both the productive power of labour and the demand for what it produces, as the ability of the community to purchase is necessarily reduced by taxes of which the burthen far exceeds the revenue they yield. The economical difficulties now felt in Victoria are not, however, due solely to the protectionist policy the Colony has long pursued. The over-haste with which it has pushed on public works and especially railways by loans so large in proportion to its immediately available resources, that they have at length led capitalists in this country to decline for the present lending the Colony more money for the same purpose, and the general want of prudence manifested by the legislature in managing its finances has no doubt contributed to bring about the check to industry which has caused the existing distress, and the disputes of labourers with their employers must have had a similar effect in even a greater degree. Making all allowances for the concurrent operation of both these disturbing influences on the labour market, the mis-direction of industry by protecting duties must still in my opinion be regarded as the main cause of that unfortunate state of things described in the telegram I have quoted.

In the other Australian Colonies the policy of Pro-tection has not, I believe, been carried to the same pitch

of extravagance as in Victoria, but it seems in all of
them to have more or less affected their financial
arrangements.   Even in New South Wales, where till
the recent change in its Government the party professing to be in favour of Free Trade has generally
been predominant, its principles have not been
thoroughly and consistently acted upon, and it appears
are now to be altogether discarded.   The practical
effect of this policy of Protection in Australia, so far
as I can judge of it from the imperfect information
I possess, has been in strict accordance with the conclusion to which reasoning leads us, that the tendency
of protecting duties is not to advance but to
retard the progress in prosperity of the communities
which adopt them.   To adhere to this policy must
therefore be regarded as a mistake, and as experience
has shown it to be unfavourable to the maintenance of
really cordial relations between the different members
of the Empire, it must also be regarded as arguing a
singular want of consistency in Colonies now much
occupied in a project of federation having for its professed object to strengthen the bond which holds them
together.

With regard to this project of federation, I greatly
doubt whether it could be successfully carried into
effect, and whether, if it were, its operation might not
prove very different from what is intended ; but as this
is not a fit opportunity of entering into so large a

question, I will only observe that even if it were
admitted to hold out as good a prospect of proving
useful as its promoters believe, still it can hardly be
supposed that its adoption could have much effect in
creating a stronger sense in the various members of
which the British Empire is made up of their having
all a real interest in maintaining its integrity and
prosperity. But this is the all-important object to
be aimed at. Improvements in the organisation of
the Empire, however well devised they might be,
cannot avail to keep it together and to make it
flourish, unless the people who live in all its widely
scattered territories have a lively sense of their
having a real common interest in its permanence and
in its welfare.

Such a sense of their having a common interest
in the welfare of the Empire can only be kept alive
in the minds of those who belong to it by their experience of its benefits; whatever therefore increases
these benefits and makes them more clear to those who
enjoy them must help to add to its security,
which must be impaired by whatever has a contrary
tendency. That their forming part of a great and
powerful Empire does confer real and important
advantages both on the United Kingdom and on all
its various dependencies seems clear from some very
obvious considerations. The security and consideration in the world now enjoyed by them all greatly

depend upon the fact of its being understood that a wrong inflicted upon any part of the Empire will be regarded as a wrong to the whole and be resented accordingly. Even to the United Kingdom the severance of its connection with the foreign dominions of the Crown would imply a serious loss both of moral and of material power, though these islands, even if they stood alone, would still constitute a powerful nation. To the Colonies the loss would be far greater ; even the strongest and most prosperous of them has not yet attained to such strength as to be able to rely upon being always able to protect itself from injury, and we have only to look to what is going on in the world around us to be convinced that unprovoked injuries by strong to much weaker nations, which were so common in ruder ages, are even now by no means impossible. Every British subject also, in whatever part of the world he may happen to be, finds that his being entitled to that character ensures to him a consideration and respect for his rights which he could not otherwise command. It is also a great advantage to him that in every part of the Empire he finds himself at home : Englishmen, Scotchmen, or Irishmen in Canada, Australia, or any other Colony have all the rights of colonists, who in like manner enjoy in the United Kingdom the same rights as ourselves ; they may sit in Parliament, and enter into any branch of the services of the State as freely as their fellow-subjects natives of these islands. This close union between them is useful to the people both of this country and of the Colonies; to the former it affords a much needed field for enterprise and for employment, without giving up the power of returning to their native land and to their relations when they have acquired adequate means, or of establishing themselves permanently in a new home without the estrangement from their old one and its associations which would result from their becoming subjects of an alien Government. To the colonist it affords similar advantages, with the additional one that it tends to raise the general tone of the society in which they live by adding to it either as temporary sojourners or as permanent settlers educated natives of the United Kingdom, bringing with them English ideas and English habits of living.

To use whatever means they possess in order to secure the continuance and the increase of these great advantages now enjoyed by all the subjects of the Queen from the maintenance of the Empire is the obvious duty both of the Imperial Government which has charge of its general interests, and of the Governments of those Colonies which are entrusted with the management of their own affairs by representative institutions. This duty will only be rightly performed when the measures of all these Governments are wisely

directed to promote the general welfare of the whole
Empire, in no case betraying the influence of a selfish
desire to promote the separate interest of any one of
the communities composing it without considering
how it may affect the common good of them all.   It
cannot be said of either the Imperial or the Colonial
Governments that they have been uniformly administered in this spirit.

The conduct of both shows, on the contrary, clear
signs of their having failed to appreciate as they ought
the importance of maintaining the integrity of the
Empire, and of acting for this purpose with a sincere
and judicious regard for the common interest.   A
careful consideration of the transactions of the last
forty years would, as I believe, amply prove the truth
of this assertion, but I will not here attempt to
state my reasons for this belief. I will content
myself with affirming my conviction that it is
correct, and also that nothing would tend so
much to improve the present state of feeling both
at home and in the colonies on this subject as
the adoption of the policy of Free Trade as that
of the whole British Empire, which would do far
more than the mere abandonment of Protection
by Canada to lead the United States to adopt the
same course.   Should this result be brought about,
what would be gained by it for the welfare of the
world defies calculation.   It would at once produce a

great improvement in the commercial relations of the United States with this country and with British North America, and thus remove what may hereafter prove to be serious causes of difference between two great English-speaking nations, and would give them a strong common interest in maintaining the peace of the world. The adoption of a Free Trade policy by the two foremost of industrial and trading communities would also before long render it difficult for other nations to abstain from following their example, and we might not unreasonably hope for the early abolition of the noxious restrictions which now impede the free intercourse of the various families of the human race. The blessing that would thus be conferred upon them all can hardly be over-estimated. Commerce is evidently designed by Providence to be a powerful instrument for promoting the welfare of mankind. It is the means by which all the nations of the earth, with their variety of climates and of soils, and of fitness for carrying on different kinds of industry should be enabled to exchange with each other whatever of the innumerable articles that contribute to the comfort and enjoyment of men each can produce best and most easily, and thus the abundance of these things which every separate community can obtain would be largely increased. Commerce, in rendering this great service to the peoples of the world, ought also to dispel the idea so generally entertained by them in the early stages of society, that strangers are necessarily enemies, and should teach them that it is the interest as well as the duty of all the different families of the human race to act towards each other with justice and as friends. Commerce ought to produce these beneficent results, but owing to the perversity and selfishness of mankind it has only done so very partially. In past times it has been too commonly carried on for the mere purpose of getting gain by any means by which it can be won, whether just or unjust, and it is still far from having entirely ceased to be so. Nations, under the hateful influence of commercial jealousy, have acted towards each other in a manner opposed alike to their own true interest and to the plainest principles of religion. In their blind desire to secure advantages for themselves without regard to the claims or the welfare of others, they have assumed that what another nation gained by selling them its goods was lost by themselves, and to avert this imaginary loss they have resorted to the system of protective duties on imports from their neighbours, not understanding that the only trade between nations which is really and permanently beneficial is that which is profitable to both parties.

In the history of the world since Europe emerged from barbarism we find but too abundant proofs of the evils which this spirit of selfishness has brought upon civilised nations. It has been the fertile source of

jealousies and animosities, sometimes even leading
directly or indirectly to war with all its horrors. The
general abandonment of the system of Protection and
the adoption of the policy of Free Trade would go far
towards checking the spirit of selfishness and of trading
jealousy, and towards improving not only the commercial but the other relations of nations with each
other. Such a change would indeed be a happy one
for the world, and the Ministers who are entrusted
with the government of this country have it in their
power to assist in bringing it about. To do so is a
worthy object for their efforts, but it is not by trying
to recommend a more liberal commercial policy to
other countries, or by pressing upon them unasked
advice, that good is likely to be done. Experience
proves that all action of this kind has the very opposite
effect from that which it is intended to produce, and
that advice offered by this country to another as to
how it may best manage its affairs for its own interest
is generally attributed to a selfish motive, and is
therefore seldom acted upon. It is by its example in
using customs duties solely for the purpose of revenue,
without reference to what duties may be imposed on
British goods by nations from which supplies of what
we want are received, and by returning avowedly and
completely to the policy successfully pursued from
1846 to 1860, and accordingly strictly abstaining from all interference or negotiation with foreign

Powers as to the duties they may impose on imports from this country, that a powerful influence might, I am persuaded, be exercised by our Government on the course taken by other nations with regard to trade.

THE END.

www.ingramcontent.com/pod-product-compliance
Lightning Source LLC
Chambersburg PA
CBHW021524270326
41930CB00008B/1080